ARE YOU
SUPERSTITIOUS?

ARE YOU SUPERSTITIOUS?

EDITED BY CAROLINE UPCHER

All royalties from this book will be donated to
The Chicken Shed Theatre Company
(Registered Charity No. 1012369)
and
CRUSAID
(Registered Charity No. 1011718)

FOURTH ESTATE · London

First published in Great Britain in 1996 by
Fourth Estate Limited
6 Salem Road
London, W2 4BU

A catalogue record for this book is available from
the British Library.

ISBN 1–85702–440–0

Printed in Great Britain by
Cox & Wyman Ltd, Reading, Berkshire

San Piedro fishermen, in 1954, were apt to pay attention to signs and portents other men had no inkling of. For them the web of cause and effect was invisible and simultaneously everywhere, which was why a man could sink his net with salmon one night and catch only kelp the next. Tides, currents, and winds were one thing, the force of luck another. A fisherman didn't utter the words horse, pig, or hog on the deck of a gill-netter, for to do so was to bring bad weather down around his head or cause a line to foul in his propeller. Turning a hatch cover upside down brought a southwest storm, and bringing a black suitcase on board meant snarled gear and twisted webbing. Those who harmed seagulls risked the wrath of ship ghosts, for gulls were inhabited by the spirits of men who had been lost at sea in accidents. Umbrellas, too, were bad business, as were broken mirrors and the gift of a pair of scissors. On board a purse seiner only a greenhorn would ever think to trim his fingernails while sitting on a seine pile, or hand a shipmate a bar of soap as opposed to dropping it into his washbasin, or cut the bottom end off a can of fruit. Bad fishing and bad weather could result from any of these.

From *Snow Falling on Cedars* by David Guterson (Bloomsbury, £5.99, © 1994 by David Guterson)

The help of the following people in putting together *Are You Superstitious?* is gratefully acknowledged:

Louise Allen-Jones
Virginia Bonham Carter
Jan Boxshall

Cartoons by Daviz

I must always take four swallows from a drink at any one time or, if I'm particularly thirsty, sixteen swallows (four times four) – of course, taking care to finish the drink on a fourth swallow.

DAVIZ
Cartoonist

CONTENTS

Note

All descriptions of contributors' occupations are
worded as they specifically requested.

Introduction

If asked 'Are you superstitious' very few people find themselves able to answer yes without hesitation. Those who are genuinely not superstitious tend to find the fact that you have asked such a question suspicious in itself. Are you one of those weirdos? Others apologise profusely because they think for some reason that, if they're not superstitious, it means they're boring.

The most common reaction is to say 'No'. Then, after a slight pause, 'but of course I never walk under ladders or do anything on Friday the thirteenth, and I always touch wood and salute magpies'. Yet they say they're not superstitious.

Truly superstitious people, whether they know it or not, have their own idiosyncratic beliefs and routines, lucky habits based on well-known superstitions and adapted to their own peculiar use.

To compile *Are You Superstitious?* – royalties to be donated to charity – we sent questionnaires to over four hundred people, targeting individuals and specific professional groups, asking them to donate a superstition (their reply could also include stating that they weren't superstitious). It was not our intention to publish a reference book or a dictionary of superstitions, but more to discover the contributors' particular quirks and, in the case of celebrities, to find out who was or wasn't superstitious. Less than fifty per cent replied and from those who did, it was not always easy to determine which groups were undeniably superstitious.

All chefs, restaurateurs and food writers said they weren't, but on the strength of Terence Conran's reply alone, should we assume that all designers are not superstitious? With the exception of Koo Stark, who treasures the Blessing Cord given to her by the Dalai Lama, none of the photographers who replied were superstitious, but is this typical of all photographers? And just because we only heard from Clapham police station that *they* weren't, does this mean the police are not superstitious?

Three groups came across as being predominantly superstitious: jockeys, writers and the homeless. And, in an indirect way, a fourth group: families. Superstitions seem to be handed down through generations. Grandmothers in particular tend to play an important role in ensuring superstitions are absorbed and adhered to, even if they are not believed. I have always suspected that my own grandmother made them up, since as a child there was very little I could do without some sort of superstitious condition being attached to it.

We were never allowed to start anything on a Friday, for instance, because that meant it would never be finished. This is particularly hard when a new television serial, a Ruth Rendell for example, begins on a Friday. I have solved this by taping the first part and watching it on another night. My mother has also pointed out that anyone who buys a lottery ticket on a Friday can't possibly win. Cutting one's toenails on a Friday is also, apparently, lethal.

You must never cry on your birthday otherwise you'll cry all the year round.

If you see a hearse you must cross your fingers until you see a four-legged animal, otherwise you'll be the next person in the hearse. My mother once saw a hearse while driving out of London with three children in the car. We were on the way to the races at Newmarket, and she drove with her fingers crossed all the way there because the first four-legged animal we saw was on the racecourse.

If you see a magpie you have to salute it and

shout: 'Good morning, Mr Magpie, seven, six, five, four, three, two, one, good morning, good morning, good morning!' This is quite fun to do if you are under ten but fearfully embarrassing if you are middle-aged and within hearing distance of others. It can also become rather boring if there is a flock of the wretched things since you have to salute each and every one of them.

If you spill salt you have to throw it over your shoulder, not once, but three times, and if you see someone else spill some you are obliged to see they do the same otherwise you will share in their bad luck. Mercifully I am very short-sighted and therefore miss a fair amount of salt spilling, otherwise I would no doubt have been thrown out of numerous restaurants by now for causing a nuisance.

If you drop a knife or a spoon (forks don't count, don't ask me why) you must never pick it up yourself or you will receive a terrible disappointment. However, the person who does pick it up will receive a wonderful surprise. This becomes a problem if you happen to be clumsy and are on your own for a period of time with very little cutlery.

The list of my family superstitions would fill another twenty pages, and it wouldn't include the normal everyday superstitions which are par for the course.

If you have any particular superstitions, or if you belong to a particular group which you feel has not been well represented, if at all, in *Are You Superstitious?* do please let us know by filling out the form at the back of the book and returning it to me at Fourth Estate Limited, 6 Salem Road, London W2 4BU. Your superstitions will be included in our next book, *Are You Superstitious Too?*, the proceeds from which will go to CRUSAID and to The Big Issue Foundation for the homeless.

Donate a superstition now!

Caroline Upcher

About the Charities

All royalties from this book will be shared between the following charities.

CRUSAID is the national fundraising charity for AIDS in the UK and depends entirely on voluntary donations. Since it was started ten years ago CRUSAID has distributed over £7.5 million for hospice care and housing, for counselling and support for education and awareness. In addition CRUSAID manages the national Hardship Fund offering relief to men, women and children in dire financial need as a result of AIDS.
Registered Charity No 1011718.

THE CHICKEN SHED THEATRE COMPANY, born in a North London barn and former chicken shed in 1974, aims to produce challenging, innovative and entertaining work through a new and exciting approach based on the belief that any young person who wants to perform has the ability and the right to do so. Chicken Shed provides a stimulating environment for performers and helps develop skills in the areas of dance, drama, music and mime, as well as direction, script writing and technical management. The range of individuality in Chicken Shed's work contributes a new dimension to theatre.

The company has played to packed auditoriums including Sadler's Wells, the Royal Albert Hall and the Piccadilly Theatre, as well as running education projects in schools, colleges and day centres. Registered Charity No 1012369.

ACTORS

I utterly disapprove of superstitions of any kind so I am ashamed to admit that when I am working in the theatre, I:

1. Never quote from or name 'the Scottish play'.

2. Never whistle in the dressing room (or if I do, I immediately go outside, turn round three times then knock before re-entering).

Ridiculous!

JANE ASHER

Actress and writer

ARE YOU SUPERSTITIOUS?

I'm afraid I am a stranger to superstition.
In fact I defy it. I walk under ladders and quote
Macbeth non-stop. So far neither loads of bricks
nor nameless catastrophes have ensued.

SIMON CALLOW

Actor

I never pick my nose during Lent.

RUPERT EVERETT

Actor

I would risk being run over on a road rather than walk under a ladder, and always say 'Good morning, sir' and spit if I see a lone magpie.

Lucky number: seven.

Lucky day: Friday thirteenth – but I wouldn't fly on it.

GERALDINE JAMES

Actress

I'm not superstitious, just devotional.

On the last night of the month I say 'Rabbits' before midnight, then through the silence I say my prayers and remember my blessings and shortcomings. My first spoken word after midnight has to be 'Hares'.

SARAH MILES

Occupation: 'just Sarah Miles'

AGENTS

I would *never* sit thirteen at the same table.

GILL COLERIDGE

Literary agent, clients include
Lynda La Plante (books),
Marina Warner, Anthony Holden

ARE YOU SUPERSTITIOUS?

I won't walk under ladders.

CHRIS OWEN

Director, Elite Premier Model Agency

Never bring may (hawthorn) blossom into the house.

When you hear a dog baying and howling in the distance it means someone in the family is going to die.

SUSAN RODGERS

Agent, clients include
Danny Boyle *(Trainspotting)*,
Lynda La Plante (scripts), Peter Hall

If she saw a magpie, my mother would not speak until she saw a nun or a black and white dog.

DEBORAH ROGERS

Literary agent, clients include
Kazuo Ishiguro, Ian McEwan,
Hanif Kureishi and David Malouf

I can only sleep with a particular tiny weeny oblong pillow with embroidered lace, otherwise I have nightmares.

CAROLE WHITE

Model agent

ANTIQUE
DEALERS

Antique dealers will not sell witches' balls, which traditionally were kept for keeping an eye on customers. They are made of mirrored glass and can be hung from the ceiling.

To get round this a dealer will sell the paper the ball is wrapped in – and charge nothing for the actual ball.

LOUISE BANNISTER

Antique dealer

ARTISTS

No.

DAVID HOCKNEY
Artist

ASTROLOGERS

ARE YOU SUPERSTITIOUS?

I'm not superstitious.

Astrology teaches you not to be superstitious. Legitimate astrologers do not believe that life is predestined. An astrological chart is a framework for the future, a series of choices, crossroads and potentials. That is a horoscope.

It is up to each and every one of us to fill in the fine detail. That is free will.

To be superstitious is to believe that external forces have control over our lives.

Astrologers believe that the planets *influence* our lives - as opposed to *controlling* them. I believe that we are all responsible for our own lives.

The planets indicate what we could be. What we become depends upon us.

SALLY BROMPTON

Astrologer

Perhaps because many people think astrology is based on superstition, it is generally assumed that astrologers are superstitious. But I've never been remotely given to rabbits' feet or concerned about broken mirrors. This foot-loose attitude must have been too much for the fates, because they saw fit to equip me with nothing less than a sleek black cat – one that was pre-named Sybil. I was living in Los Angeles at the time, and it began when a neighbour left her, as a six-month-old kitten, for me to cat-sit. The neighbour never returned, and while I would never have deliberately acquired a black cat, she quickly became part of the household, and of my image.

I try to maintain a businesslike manner. Sybil thought otherwise. Because writing took up a smaller proportion of my time, I saw more private clients. Generally she would wait until they were seated, then stroll in to conduct an inspection. She managed, from her foot-high feline stature, to look down at mere humans, quickly reducing most to the level of subjects. Once they knew their place, she would depart, leaving them to me.

She became a legend; no visit was complete without an audience with Sybil. Travellers would return with black cat-motif souvenirs.

ARE YOU SUPERSTITIOUS?

Most of all she reminded me that even non-superstitious astrologers can derive benefit from the spell cast by a small black cat.

SHELLEY VON STRUNCKEL

Astrologer

ARE YOU SUPERSTITIOUS?

I only write in black ink or pencil as everything I have written in blue ink in recent months has either been cancelled or not gone according to plan.

JESSICA WILSON

Student astrologer/assistant to
Shelley von Strunckel

Interestingly the writer Muriel Spark revealed on BBC2's Bookmark *that she has to write with a black biro, which only she is allowed to use. If someone accidentally touches it, she immediately has to throw it out of the window and use another.*

BOOKMAKERS

When I'm running real bad I throw my underwear out of the window wherever I'm living. If I'm feeling very civilised I might put it in the incinerator.

New York bookmaker
wishing to remain anonymous

BROADCASTERS, COMPOSERS AND TELEVISION ENTERTAINERS

No, touch wood.

CLIVE ANDERSON

Barrister and broadcaster

My lucky number is four – or, indeed, any even numbers.

When I lock up the house at night, I always have to go back and check each door, maybe as many as three or four times.

When I was a child I always used to have a square of cloth called Tatty. I couldn't do anything without Tatty. If it was lost my parents knew they would have no peace until it was found. Tatty became rather smelly because I hated it to be washed. Tatty had a particular smell and if it was washed the smell was never quite the same.

In a way, Tatty was the forerunner for a particular earpiece that I wear during broadcasts for television. If I don't have it, I become quite unsettled and am quite sure things are going to go wrong.

MICHAEL BERKELEY

Composer and broadcaster.

I have worn the same bathrobe in my dressing room for *Surprise Surprise* since the very first series.

It's covered in patches but I refuse to get another one because the day I stop wearing it the show will be a miss.

CILLA BLACK
Television entertainer

ARE YOU SUPERSTITIOUS?

1. Never pass salt from hand to hand.

2. Do not look at the new moon through glass (difficult because I wear spectacles).

3. My lucky number: too important to be revealed.

LOYD GROSSMAN

Broadcaster

I believe seeing one magpie is very unlucky and I go mad looking for another as seeing two is supposed to be lucky.

CAROLINE HOOK
Chat show host Mrs Merton

CHEFS,
RESTAURATEURS
AND
FOOD WRITERS

I am not superstitious to the point that I opened the Manoir aux Quat' Saisons on Friday the thirteenth 1984!

RAYMOND BLANC

Chef and patron

No, sorry.

SOPHIE GRIGSON

Food writer

I'm not at all superstitious, or don't think of myself as so, but the 'blood and bandages' connotation of red and white flowers together makes me actively dislike the combination, even though red and white is a great combo for anything other than flowers.

PRUE LEITH
Restaurateur and food writer

CRICKET

In cricket, the number 111 is called a 'Nelson' and is regarded as unlucky.

STEPHEN GREEN

Curator, Marylebone Cricket Club

This superstition may be to do with the fact that the number 111 looks like three wickets. There is an umpire who always stands on one leg when the score reaches 111.

DESIGNERS

No.

TERENCE CONRAN

Designer

FAMILIES

The Fillary Family

The Fillary family's superstitions were provided by Mrs Betty Fillary of the Institute of Plumbing.

With plumbing, there aren't really superstitions, but you can always be prepared for what looks like a real challenge to be solved in an uncanny way. I once went to a house I had never been to before and found that the connections were almost impossible to reach. Without knowing why I did it, I went straight to the owner's shed and immediately found two blowlamps. I placed them in a position where the heat could sweat the joints to release them and suddenly I was able to do the job.

TERRY FILLARY

Plumber

ARE YOU SUPERSTITIOUS?

Last year I had a very awkward job with a huge boiler. I needed another plumber to help me but he let me down at the last minute so I had to go on my own. When I got to the job, I looked at it, sat down, poured myself a cup of tea from my flask and wondered what I was going to do. It looked hopeless. Suddenly I asked myself what would my grandfather, Ted Fillary, have done to tackle the problem and then I knew what to do. I got out my tools and cut the boiler up into sections, and it worked.

PAUL FILLARY

Plumber

The Puttnam Family

Superstitions are often handed down through generations. The Puttnam family – husband and wife David and Patricia and their son Alexander – explain their superstitions.

My paternal grandmother was deeply superstitious. When she lived with my mother during World War II she passed these superstitions on. I was born into this family and we survived the bombing, hence the deep abiding belief developed by my mother, and later by myself, in my grandmother's unbelievably banal series of superstitions.

1. Don't walk under ladders.

2. Do not pass on the stairs.

3. If you give anyone anything sharp – e.g. scissors or a penknife – you must be paid for it and receive a coin in exchange.

4. It is potentially lethal to step on the crack in the pavement.

5. Knock wood.

We survived the war, therefore these superstitions must be true!

DAVID PUTTNAM

Film producer

ARE YOU SUPERSTITIOUS?

There are moments when I suddenly remember that someone I love could be in a potentially dangerous situation. I imagine the worst fatality occurring and I cannot leave that thought to linger without pushing into the distance in my mind with both hands outstretched until it disappears into a white light.

PATRICIA PUTTNAM

When I was a little boy I could not leave the house until the cuffs of the jersey of my school uniform were absolutely equal. Socks, too.

I always take the stairs two at a time so if I get to a landing and there's only one step left, I have to jump to the next flight of stairs.

When I am really hoping for something to happen, it will happen if I beat the bus or a particular car in the traffic to the traffic lights.

In Italy, whenever you toast someone all the guests have to look each other in the eye and all the glasses must touch.

When I was living in Moscow studying conducting at the Moscow State Conservatory,

ARE YOU SUPERSTITIOUS?

people did not leave for a long journey without
first sitting down together, putting down their
bags and being silent for a few minutes.

ALEXANDER PUTTNAM

Conductor

This superstition was handed down from my grandmother in Puglia, Southern Italy. If I am frightened I make the sign of the devil's horns with my index finger and my little finger and touch metal.

BRUNO SEMERARO

Housekeeper

FASHION

I am not normally superstitious; however, I have a problem tempting fate.

ALLY CAPELLINO

Fashion designer

No.

BETTY JACKSON

Fashion designer

Cutting Room Superstitions

No whistling in the workroom before a collection – it's very bad luck and the show will not be a success.

If you drop a pair of scissors on the floor and they land open, facing somebody, that person will marry.

If you drop a pair of scissors on the floor and they land with one of the blades stuck in the floor, then someone in the room will die.

If you blow up a paper bag (or even a crisp packet) and burst it in the workroom, then someone will get the sack.

Never unpick a garment on a Monday morning before noon, or you will be unpicking it for the rest of the week.

If you make your own wedding dress, you should never quite finish it. Let someone else sew the last stitch to ensure a happy marriage.

TOMASZ STARZEWSKI

Fashion designer

FITNESS
TRAINERS

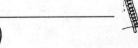

If a pigeon takes a dump on me while I am out power-walking with a client, this brings good luck.

LIZE VAN DER WALT

Fitness trainer

HAIRDRESSERS

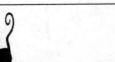

Sometimes I'm superstitious. I never walk under scaffolding and always say good morning to magpies.

A. M. BRYANT

Hairdresser, session stylist for
The Face and *ID* magazines

No.

NICKY CLARKE

Hairdresser

I am a bit superstitious. I don't walk under ladders or put new shoes on the table.

LINDA EVANS

Director, Mascolo PR

I am mildly superstitious. In Italy, where my family originate, the number seventeen, instead of thirteen, is terribly unlucky.

I make sure that I avoid anything major on Friday the seventeenth, which seems to confuse lots of people.

ANTHONY MASCOLO

British Hairdresser of the Year;
International Artistic Director, Toni & Guy

I feel that if I broke a mirror, I would get seven years' bad luck – and if I see one magpie I salute it so I don't get sorrow.

SACHA MASCOLO

Hairdresser, Toni & Guy

THE
HOMELESS

ARE YOU SUPERSTITIOUS?

We are especially grateful to the Big Issue writing group who gather every Wednesday morning in Clerkenwell and write for two hours (as well as various other things!).

On the morning of Wednesday, 31 January 1996, they were asked to write down their superstitions. When they had finished, before handing them in to be included in Are You Superstitious?, *they gave a reading, acting out the pages that follow.*

Half of the proceeds of Are You Superstitious Too?, *to which we hope you will contribute a superstition by completing the form on page 143, will be donated to the Big Issue Foundation for the homeless (Registered Charity No 1049077).*

I never put money or notes on a bed. It's unlucky,
and it means you'll lose it.

ROBYN HEATON
Big Issue writing group

If I see someone has left the lid open on the
photocopier, I have to close it otherwise doom is
imminent.

DERMOT McPARTLAND
Advertising & Marketing Director, *The Big Issue*

ARE YOU SUPERSTITIOUS?

A gothic-looking church on Leman Street, London E1, is on the left-hand side of my window view from the Beacon Hostel. It's late October and I'm playing my keyboard – unconnected melody, chord progressions. It's after midnight. I'm looking out of my window, staring rather vacantly.

Suddenly a multi-coloured image, a body, flashes past my windowsill, falling. I run to the window and look down in shock. Nothing.

Next door my neighbours are still awake so I go and tell them what happened, only to learn that some poor bastard had jumped from the third floor only a few months before.

Apparently it was roughly the same time: 12.40 am.

The victim's brother turned up the very next day while I was in the communal laundry room but he only repeated what the neighbours had already told me. There was no scream, no ruckus beforehand, the guy simply jumped.

Since then, on the twenty-sixth of every month, I've lit a candle, prayed and played a few chords and at about the same time I always see the image of that boy's body. Dave, only twenty-three.

ANDY AUKER

88

I will never sleep with my body crossing the direction in which the floorboards have been placed. I also never sleep lengthways facing a doorway. Whenever I've done this in the past I haven't been able to sleep or I've had disturbing nightmares. For that reason it's turned into my superstition.

ARWYN CARMODY

Aged twenty-two, homeless on and off
since he was fifteen

Am I superstitious?

Well, basically, no. The simple fact remains, however, that if someone believes something it is true for them. There are old rhymes such as 'Rain before seven, clear before eleven' which are true and do work. Of course, these things must be tested by your own experience or you may end up believing everything.

As well as superstitions there are spiritual laws, if you aren't afraid of the term, which also apply and which can only be discovered on a scientific basis. Everyone has heard the expression 'What goes around, comes around', but not everyone knows this is related to the Karmic law 'what you give out, you will get back threefold' - although it generally isn't quite as simple as that.

Finally: money. Did you know that giving ten per cent of your money to the poor (and not to the National Lottery) is a recipe for continually increasing your wealth? Rubbish? Superstition? Try it for a year and see. That is Spiritual Science.

CONRAD – BOLD COUNSEL

This is a superstition from my gambling days when I used to be almost compulsive about betting on horses.

I often used to pick up a penny or any coin I saw on the pavement. My bets for that day were nearly always lucrative. My luck increased greatly. Was it just coincidence or did that coin I picked up bring me luck?

Then if someone in the betting shop asked for a couple of quid, and I gave it to them, even if I was on a winning streak, my luck would change drastically for the worse. Strange but true!

So it must be advisable for street beggars or buskers to pick up every coin donated. You're asking for trouble if you don't!

DAVE DUNCAN

My mother was always saying, 'I'm so happy, it can't last.'

When I became homeless I saw her saying this whenever I laughed. I had a premonition: it won't last. I'm frightened now of being happy.

FATMA DURMUSH

Turkish family, born in England.
Homeless for three months
after she ran away
from an arranged marriage.

My superstitions mainly come from drug use. For instance, if I go out stealing, I know I'll get caught if I don't go back into the shop straight after taking whatever it was I took. I have to wander around casually and then I leave.

Another superstition as a homeless junkie is not buying syringes before I buy the smack. I like to have all my paraphernalia in the right place. Also, if, for example, I know I can buy a £15 bag for £13, then I must buy it for £14.

J. HURBIS

Ex-punk, aged thirty,
homeless for many years

The city of discovery in Scotland is Dundee. The Law Hill is filled with spirits, phantoms, mystery.

I was sleeping rough on the hill huddled between the trees when a voice said from somewhere, 'What are you doing here?'

I looked around but there was no one in sight. I began to feel nervous and intensely frightened. I caught a glimpse of a woman in white and she said 'leave my domain or die tonight'. Then she disappeared.

Ever since then, when I'm sleeping on the streets or in forests, I always get a sense that someone will tell me to move away.

K. JACK

Aged twenty-one,
homeless since he was sixteen

In Africa, when someone is homeless, there is a superstition that that person must have done something seriously wrong to deserve his or her fate.

The locals say that the person's neighbours or enemies are concocting voodoo against them and the gods are against them.

The homeless victim then starts visiting voodoo chiefs and trying to appease the gods to make their situation better.

KUMBI JOHNSON

Nigerian family, born in London;
homeless for three years

My grandmother always says:

'Do not put black on a bed because someone will die.'

'Do not cut your toenails and fingernails on the carpet.'

'Every time I have an itchy palm I receive money soon afterwards.'

JEANETTE JU-PIERRE

I will never walk under a ladder.

If I spill salt, I throw it over my left shoulder with my right hand. I don't know why. It's something that's been handed down, like not putting shoes on a bed or a table.

GEORGIE MAC

Homeless for four years

I don't believe in superstitions because I believe in God.

HARRY O.

Never leave nail clippings around. They will give others power over you.
Never kick a black cat. It will haunt you forever.
Always tell bees what's happened in your family.
Do not disturb bumble bees. If you do your home will be in jeopardy.

KEITH RAMSDEN-MELLOR

'Is that where the expression "The powers that be" comes from?'

HARRY O.

An old Romany superstition is that around the camp fire, if you burn your finger on a pot or a kettle you must wet your thumb and index finger with spit and pinch your ear lobe. Even now, when I'm using smack, if I burn my finger I do the thumb trick.

GARRY ORANGE

JOCKEYS

ARE YOU SUPERSTITIOUS?

These superstitions were contributed by John Buckingham, former jockey 1957-71 and winner of the 1967 Grand National; now a jockey's valet.

ARE YOU SUPERSTITIOUS?

With a sport like ours I think people are more likely to be superstitious. People used to ask me if I was superstitious and I used to say no but deep down I think I am because I always salute a lone magpie seven times. One for sorrow, two for joy, three for a girl, four for a boy, five for silver, six for gold, seven for a story never to be told.

When I was riding I never left the weighing room without chewing gum and I used to spit it out just before we jumped off. I used to say it was because I wanted to keep my mouth moist and I bought Wrigley's spearmint in big packets, but it was a kind of superstition. Even if I had three rides in a day I'd always have a piece of gum in my mouth when I got on the horse, then I'd canter down to the start and spit it out before we jumped off.

There was one time years ago when I was a stable lad and a friend and I were in the back of the horse box going to the races somewhere. There was a superstition that if you saw an ambulance you had to hold your collar, and hold your breath, until you saw a four-legged animal. Well, we saw an ambulance and there we were holding our breath and clinging on to our collars, but we couldn't see an animal anywhere. After half an hour we happened to look round and of course there were two in the horse box. We were looking out of the window for a sheep or something out in the fields when literally within a yard of us there was a horse's head.

There was a horse called Reynoldstown which won the Grand National two years running. The first year Major Furlong trained him and his son rode him. Unfortunately this was during the war years and his son was killed, and the next year the horse was ridden by Fulke Walwyn. On the way up to Liverpool that first year they saw a funeral and they said 'Ah, that's luck, we'll win the National today.' It's a common superstition, so they say, that if you see a funeral it'll bring you luck. The following year they went up with the same horse and they drove round Liverpool until they saw a funeral and they won again.

Deep down I think I must be superstitious up to a point. The day I was asked to ride Foinavon in the Grand National was a Wednesday in 1967. I was getting dressed to go to my uncle's funeral when the phone went. I was putting my tie on, a black tie, so I stopped and went to answer the phone and was asked to ride the horse in the National. So there was the funeral connection again.

Jockeys hate to wear new silks. They always get their valet or someone else to jump on them before they put them on. They've got to get them dirty at some point so it might as well be before they put them on.

There's a jockey who doesn't feel comfortable riding a certain woman owner's horse unless she is wearing a particular blue and green hat. When he rides into the paddock, if she's not wearing that hat he doesn't feel lucky.

David Nicholson never goes racing without red socks on.

If ever a jockey I look after called Graham Thorner had anything new – new boots, new saddle, new pair of britches – he'd always have to put them on a kid, a young lad having his first ride, and let him have a ride in them so they'd been worn before he used them.

ARE YOU SUPERSTITIOUS?

There are a lot of jockeys who wear their underpants until they're falling apart. They don't say anything but it's probably because they think they're lucky. We said to Luke Harvey the other day, 'Look, Luke, the bottom's falling out of these pants, don't you think you ought to throw them away?' 'Oh,' he said, 'they'll last another season.'

I tie the silk under the cap and a long time ago there was a jockey who always said, every time I tied it, 'Bit tighter.' I never said anything to him but I suspect it was something he had to say for luck. Now there's another just started saying the same thing. 'Bit tighter.'

There's another jockey who, every time he goes in the weighing room, makes a little sound, and I make the same sound back to him. We've never said anything about it but we always do it. He has to do it, and if I see him first I have to do it. It's just one of those things.

JOHN BUCKINGHAM

Jockey's valet

NANNIES

Walking under a ladder and the number thirteen are unlucky.

NANNY BRAND

Children's nurse

ARE YOU SUPERSTITIOUS?

When I was a child I copied my godmother
throwing three pinches of spilled salt over my left
shoulder using my right hand. I did it because my
godmother did it. It was nothing to do with the
superstition, which is possibly to do with Lot's
wife who turned into a pillar of salt. I think a lot
of superstitions have their roots in the Bible. Like
Friday the thirteenth being unlucky – I suppose
it's because Jesus died on a Friday. He had twelve
disciples and he made thirteen. I'm only guessing,
but it seems likely.

NANNY SMITH

Children's nurse

NEWSPAPERS
AND
MAGAZINES

When reading books, I always try to avoid leaving off where the digits of the page number add up to thirteen. For example, reading a novel on the train this morning, I was coming dangerously close to page 148 as we hurtled towards Waterloo. It was the usual dilemma: do I stop now, safe at page 147, or steam ahead and risk all manner of goblinorama by not getting to 149? As it happened, because of a loud, distracting conversation next to me, I didn't make it past the dreaded page. But rather than leave my bookmark there all day, I carried on reading during my short Tube journey – something I don't usually do. I'm still alive as a result.

TONY BARRELL

Deputy Chief Sub-Editor
on a national colour supplement

ARE YOU SUPERSTITIOUS?

My lucky number is thirty-two.

I never walk under ladders. I would rather be run over than walk under a ladder.

I wear lucky cufflinks (yellow and blue dots) on special days.

I touch the lintels of doorways for luck.

NICHOLAS COLERIDGE

Author, publisher,
Managing Director of Condé Nast

I am not superstitious, except when I travel. And I do touch wood.

ALEXANDRA SHULMAN

Editor of *Vogue*

PHOTOGRAPHERS

ARE YOU SUPERSTITIOUS?

Photographer Helmut Newton is superstitious – but his wife, June, isn't.

I like to travel and to marry on the thirteenth.

HELMUT NEWTON

Photographer

No.

**JUNE NEWTON
a.k.a. ALICE SPRINGS**

Photographer

I always walk under ladders.

Having done it once accidentally with no mishaps, I concluded that to carry on tempting fate was lucky for me.

TERRY O'NEILL

Photographer

I am not superstitious because it brings bad luck
to be so!

JEAN LOUP SIEFF

Amateur photographer

The Blessing Cord given to me by His Holiness
the Dalai Lama is most important. It is a red
thread with a small knot in it which I wear around
my neck.

KOO STARK

Photographer

THE
POLICE

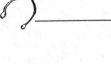

ARE YOU SUPERSTITIOUS?

I have canvassed the officers at Clapham Police
Station without any reported superstition.
Is this a police trait?

INSPECTOR R. ANTHONY

Clapham Police

STUNTMEN

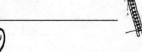

Before leaving home to do a stunt, I usually knock on the door three times. Then, when I get home and before I do anything else, I knock on the door a further three times.

Also, whenever I see a magpie I have to clap my hands to avoid bad luck. It's unfortunate that flocks of them live along the road to Pinewood Studios and it's even more difficult for me to clap my hands when I'm on my motorbike.

SIMON CRANE

Stunt co-ordinator/performer,
films include *Goldeneye*

A stunt man does not have the privilege of being superstitious. If there is a fixed date where everything fits into place for the schedule when they want me to turn a car over or fall off a building, and that date happens to be Friday the thirteenth, then I have to do it on that day.

If I could only perform a stunt with a rabbit's foot in my hand – for instance diving off a cliff doubling for Tarzan – you can see it just wouldn't work.

PETER BRAYHAM

Stunt/action co-ordinator
and 2nd Unit Director

WRITERS

Whenever I see a red-haired woman I cross the road.

To meet her!

DAN BINCHY

Writer

I'm not superstitious. But I do worry about the Beatles song 'When I'm sixty-four'.

I'm almost afraid to sing it in case I won't get there.

MAEVE BINCHY

Writer

The diamond I found in the street is not exactly a lucky charm, more something which reminds me that miracles do happen.

About twenty years ago, browsing through a street market in Dorset, I picked up a trashy-looking ring on the pavement. None of the stall-holders would claim it, so I kept it. Driving home, west, into the setting sun, it sparkled so much that I took it to a jeweller friend who said the stone was a diamond of about one carat. She reset it for me and I've worn it ever since.

CELIA BRAYFIELD

Author

ARE YOU SUPERSTITIOUS?

I am not superstitious. I walk under ladders etc.
However, I do not feel comfy unless I plant, or
have, a gum tree in my garden. Only then do I feel
the house and garden are mine.

CARMEN CALLIL

Literary critic, writer,
Chairman of the 1996 Booker Prize

ARE YOU SUPERSTITIOUS?

When I am engaged in a game of limited chance I feel jinxed if my partners indulge in premature chirping (ie gloating before the game is completely won).

ANNABEL DAVIS-GOFF

Writer and gambler,
author of *The Literary Companion To Gambling*

I don't have lucky charms etc. How it works for me is on feelings. If I do such and such then such and such is bound to happen – which is silly! These 'feelings' arise at random so they don't really fall into any category.

MARGARET FORSTER

Writer

ARE YOU SUPERSTITIOUS?

Author Frederick Forsyth isn't superstitious – but his wife Sandy is.

Alas, no, in no way.

FREDERICK FORSYTH

Author

Yes. Three nuns together in a public place presage unhappy or dire news for me.

SANDY FORSYTH

Writer

I have a lucky bead given to me years ago by a sculptor I met who lived in a remote house in Washington State.

I was impressed with this woman's courage and fortitude. She had left a stifling marriage at the age of sixty and built her little house in the wood, a house which had an atmosphere of serenity and productivity. There was a bed, a work table and an immense view of the woods.

The bead is beautiful – shaped like a woman's head. It fits into the palm of your hand. I clutch it at times when courage or concentration is needed. Recently I lent it to my daughter when she was sitting an exam. She passed.

JULIA GREGSON

Writer and journalist

My friends and I 'doom' the opposing goalkeeper at Arsenal by pointing lighted cigarettes at him. And my two-year-old son wears an Arsenal shirt around the house during home games.

Nothing is much use, though.

NICK HORNBY

Writer

Am I superstitious? Yes-ish.

Sixty-three is my lucky number. It was my primary school peg number.

I NEVER celebrate, get interested in, have anything to do with

HALLOWEEN

I don't even like to write the word.

WILLIAM HORWOOD

Best-selling novelist

ARE YOU SUPERSTITIOUS?

Never use the word 'Lucky' in the title of a play.

Never whistle in the dressing room because it's unlucky. This goes back to the days when you whistled to the men controlling the flies and the scenery, and the wrong whistle could bring the wrong one down. If you do whistle you have to leave the dressing room, turn round three times, re-enter and swear.

If you use any of the lines from Macbeth in the dressing room it is always said to be unlucky. Once again you have to leave the dressing room, turn around three times, go back in and swear.

If you go out on New Year's Eve, when you come back to your house for the first time in the New Year bring a piece of coal and some salt and the first person over the threshold should have very dark hair.

Never talk about a project or a contract before it's signed.

It's unlucky to have an empty hearse overtake you.

Don't walk under ladders.

LYNDA LA PLANTE

Writer

Cats are lucky for different things. I called one tom cat my 'literary agent'. I had good contracts while he was alive.

My current cat, KGB, picked my husband. KGB wouldn't go to bed with my other lovers but considered James to be family immediately.

My mother is visited by Korky, the premium bond cat. Anyone who strokes him wins. We've both had several £50 wins after winning nothing for twenty years. One woman comes from Spain every six months to stroke him for luck.

FIONA PITT-KETHLEY

Writer

No.

TOM STOPPARD
Playwright

No.

JOANNA TROLLOPE
Novelist

I always give money to the nun at Los Angeles Airport – and don't tell her I'm Protestant!

My lucky charm is a little dog figurine from *The Lady and the Tramp* that caught my mother's fancy the day before I was born in 1955.

LAURA VAN WORMER

Novelist

138

I am very superstitious. Absolutely! It's my Irish blood.

When I forget something I have to go back to the house every single time. Then I have to sit down, otherwise unimaginable things befall me. This has sometimes led to my missing trains and things, arguably counteracting the benefits. I have been observed by my neighbours, when I'm particularly short of time but anxious not to incur the wrath of fate, sitting briefly in the porch, which seems to work as well.

PENNY VINCENZI

Journalist and novelist

Index of Contributors

ARE YOU SUPERSTITIOUS?

ARE YOU SUPERSTITIOUS TOO?

If you would like to donate a superstition to our next book, *Are You Superstitious Too?*, please complete and sign this form and send it to Caroline Upcher, Fourth Estate, 6 Salem Road, London W2 4BU.

For every copy sold we will donate a royalty to the charities CRUSAID and The Big Issue Foundation.

Are you superstitious? YES ❑ NO ❑

If you are, please describe the superstition, lucky charm or number(s) most important to you overleaf or on a separate sheet of paper.

I agree to the entry overleaf being included in *Are You Superstitious Too?* and give Fourth Estate exclusive rights to publish or license for publication my contribution in volume book form and other printed media throughout the world.

Signed . . . .
PLEASE PRINT IN CAPITALS

Name . . . .

Address . . . .

. . . .

. . . .

Daytime telephone no . . . .

Occupation, or how you would like to be described in the book

. . . .

The Big Issue Foundation – Registered Charity No. 1049077

CRUSAID – Registered Charity No. 101171

ARE YOU SUPERSTITIOUS TOO?

PLEASE PRINT IN CAPITALS